D1558397

The author and his grandmother

THE VANDERBILTS IN MY LIFE

A PERSONAL MEMOIR BY

SHIRLEY BURDEN

Ticknor & Fields New Haven and New York 1981

Picture credits: page 12, Brown Brothers; 31, Kennedy and Company; 44-45, Brown Brothers; 64, Rensselaer County Historical Society; 134, © Karsh-Ottawa.

Designed by Murray Belsky

Library of Congress Cataloging in Publication Data

Burden, Shirley
The Vanderbilts in my life.

1. Vanderbilt family. 2. Burden, Shirley.
I. Title.
CT274.V35B87 973'.09'92 [B] 81-9012
ISBN 0-89919-049-9 AACR2

Printed in the United States of America

H 10 9 8 7 6 5 4 3 2 1

To my grandchildren

and their children

and their children

PREFACE

I never knew my great-great-grandfather, Cornelius Vanderbilt —the Commodore, as he was called—because he died thirty-one years before I was born. Many books have been written about him, many things said: some good, some bad. No one can deny the fact that he was a shrewd businessman and made a lot of money.

The Commodore would never have entered my life if it hadn't been for the deaths of my grandmother, the Commodore's granddaughter; and her daughter, Ruth Twombly. They died within a year of each other. At the time, death to me was something you read about in the obituary columns of newspapers. It wasn't a reality.

I was never very close to my grandmother, but somehow, when she and my aunt both left, there was death staring me in the face. It was then that I decided to visit the Commodore in his last resting place on Staten Island. I knew I couldn't talk to him, but I thought his presence, even in death, might straighten things out for me.

After that visit I knew I had to do this book. It wasn't easy. Books are not my strong point. Life to me is what I see and hear. And the mother I loved so much never liked the idea. I never could explain to her—yes, it is about her family and yet, it isn't. It's about the continuance of life. Along the way there are many incidents. These are the ones I will never forget.

S.C.B.

New York City
and Beverly Hills
1981

They tell a story about the Commodore when he was young that reveals more about his character than do volumes of history books. He lived with his father and mother in a house on Staten Island. What little money the family had his father held onto with an iron hand. Any money his mother was able to save she hid in their grandfather clock in the hall. She loved her son very much and would do anything for him.

One day Vanderbilt was walking along the Staten Island shore—across the bay he could see young New York. Wouldn't it be great if he could get a boat and take produce from Staten Island and sell it in New York? It didn't take him long to find a suitable boat; the next thing was to see if he could get a loan from his father to buy it. His father refused. He asked him several times, but the answer was always no. Then he went to his mother and asked if she would help.

Her answer was quite different. She emptied her hiding place in the grandfather clock and gave him all the money she had. He still didn't have enough to buy the boat so he went back to his father. I imagine by this time his father was sick of his son's persistence so he said, "You know that large field I have, covered with rocks—if you clear it in three days, I'll lend you the money." He knew as well as his son did that such a thing was impossible.

But young Vanderbilt was never the type to give up—he went to his friends and told them if they would help him clear his father's field he would take them and their girls to New York on Saturdays, free. In three days the field was cleared, and Vanderbilt got the money from his begrudging father.

Saturday arrived. Vanderbilt's boat was filled to capacity with happy girls and boys. It was a tired group that returned to the boat that evening for the voyage home to Staten Island. When Vanderbilt got half way across New York Harbor he stopped the boat and explained to his friends that, although the trip over was free, they would have to pay for the return trip.

When he died, in January 1877, he was the richest man in the United States. He left behind a wife, Sophia Johnson who was his cousin, and twelve children: four boys—William Henry, Cornelius Jeremiah, Frances, and George Washington—and eight girls—Phebe Jane, Ethelinda, Emily, Eliza, Sophia Johnson, Mary Alicia, Catherine Juliet, and Mary Louise;

a fleet of steamboats;

and a number of railroads: N.Y. and Harlem, a complex of railroad lines to Albany, a complex of railroad lines to Buffalo (which later became the N.Y. Central System), and his own private locomotive with his name on the side and his picture on the headlight.

I began my trip to see the Commodore with a ferry ride from the Battery in New York City to Staten Island. It took me twenty-five minutes. I was depressed enough when I started but the look on the deckhand's face when I arrived at Staten Island added to my depression.

COMMODORE
Bay Ridge Water & Lighterage Co Inc.
DRINKING
WATER HOSE
ONLY

On the way to the Moravian Cemetery at New Dorp, where the Commodore is buried, I came across many reminders. He hasn't been forgotten entirely.

I was told at the cemetery that the Commodore has two tombs. The first one I came to was temporary, they said. It certainly looked it. Trees were growing out through the roof. A threatening figure glared down at me from behind a shroud that covered half her face. A metal door to the tomb had disintegrated to such an extent it was flaking onto the sill below. It just couldn't be the last resting place for such an illustrious personage as the Commodore, whose last name was originally spelled Van Derbilt.

My next stop was in front of a pair of iron gates. They weren't the heavenly gates but they were very impressive. They led to a fifteen-acre plot, the last resting place for the Commodore and a number of his descendants. I walked up an overgrown road to a forest of young trees. I felt terribly alone.

In the distance I saw a small tool shed—perhaps there was life there. There wasn't. The door was locked. It stood staring at me as if to say, "Go away, only the dead live here." I agreed I wanted to be somewhere else, anyplace else, quickly. Then something caught my eye.

It wasn't a bird, or a leaf in the wind—it was a live human being, with a hat and overalls, eating a sandwich. He didn't seem startled when I approached him, with my view camera and tripod over my shoulder. He just said hello and went on eating. We had lunch together many times after that.

My first view of the Commodore's tomb affected me as if I had found Notre Dame Cathedral in the middle of the Sahara Desert. William H. Vanderbilt, the Commodore's son, must have felt, as I did, that the Commodore deserved a more impressive structure for all eternity than the temporary tomb he was first housed in, so he built him a replica of the Romanesque Chapel of Saint Giles at Arles.

Scattered among the trees there were Shepards and Sloanes and Hammonds, etc.—all descendants of the Commodore.

I watched as my gardener friend closed the gates for the night. Each morning he opened them; each evening he closed them. I wondered why—nobody was going anyplace.

My mind wandered into the past. I could hear hoofbeats in the distance. They grew louder and louder. A long line of shining carriages, drawn by beautifully groomed horses, was winding its way up the road to the Commodore's tomb. Immaculately dressed footmen, wearing high hats with rosettes on the side, sat like statues, guiding the horses. As the carriages passed, I could see men in black morning coats, with ladies beside them in black lace dresses, high, black lace collars, and black lace picture hats. They faded away as quickly as they had come. Then the road was filled with Rolls Royces—lots of them. Some were painted a deep wine color. The chauffeurs and footmen wore caps and liveries to match.

William H. Vanderbilt, the Commodore's son, inherited many of his father's traits. He increased the family fortune from one hundred million dollars to two hundred million.

He loved railroads. He had his own private train decorated with museum pieces and the most lavish brocades.

His carriage house contained

every conceivable type of carriage. He loved horses, not just to look at but to drive—fast.

Unlike his father, he was a gentle soul with very few enemies. He lived in a rather extraordinary mansion at 640 Fifth Avenue in New York City, with his wife, Maria Louisa Kissam, and his nine children: five boys—Cornelius, Allen, William Kissam, Frederick William, and George Washington—and four girls—Margaret Louisa, Emily Thorn, Florence Adele, and Eliza Osgood. The bronze doors at 640 were Barbedienne reductions of those by Ghiberti in the Baptistry at Florence. They were formerly the doors of the palace of the Prince of San Donato.

The entrance hall struck quite a different note.

After studying the living rooms, I decided I would have chosen another interior decorator.

This semiclad figure holding the lamp was, I imagine, stationed there to guide you to the second floor.

William H., I am told, enjoyed collecting art. Now I know where the phrase "Everyone to his own taste" came from.

The plants in the solarium must have been a welcome relief from all this weird grandeur.

Margaret Louisa Vanderbilt

Emily Thorne Vanderbilt

Eliza Osgood Vanderbilt

In a way, William H. Vanderbilt's four daughters were the real stars of the family. They were rich, they had social position, and they married well. They also had the Commodore's ambition.

Florence Adele Vanderbilt

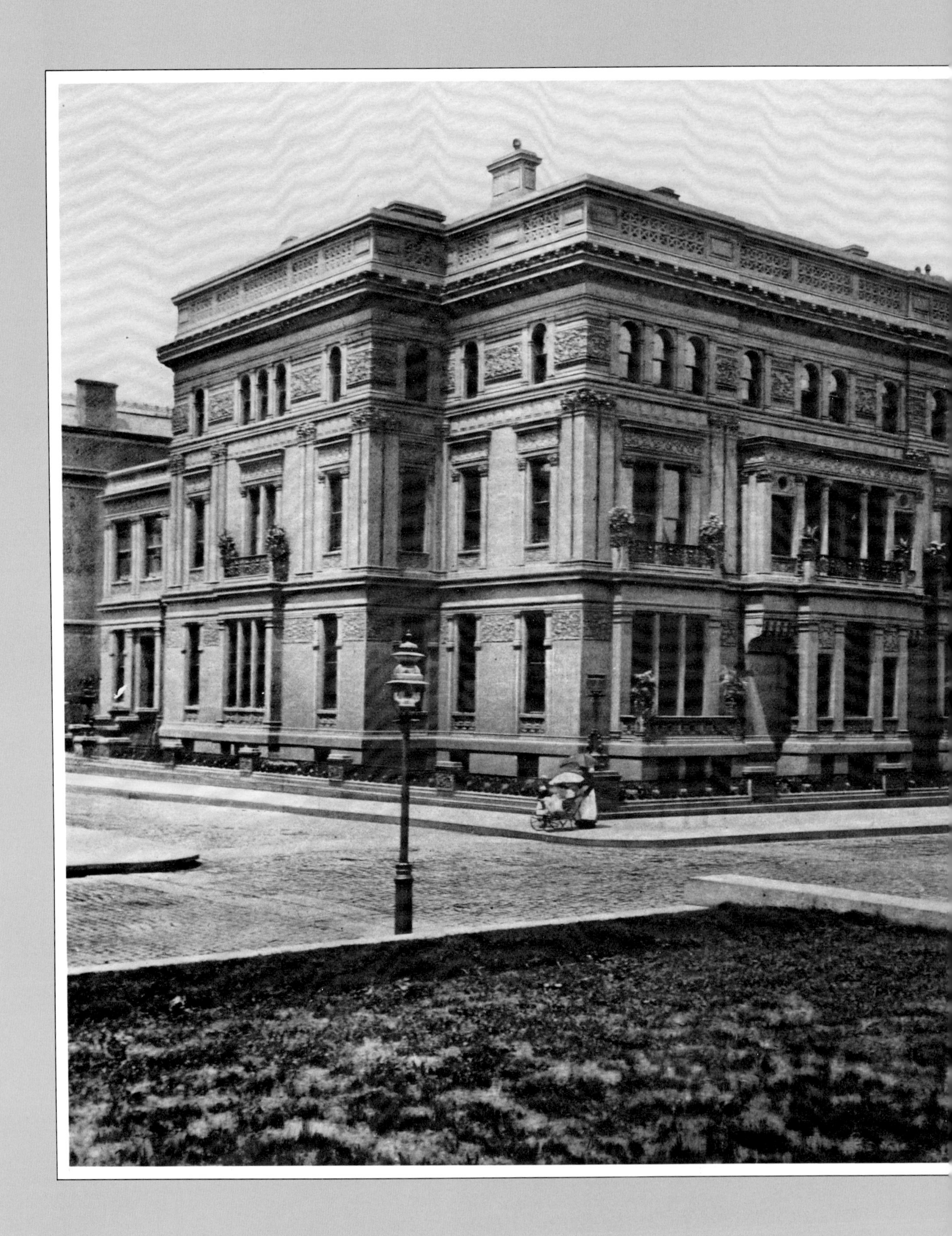

If one of them built a house with thirty guest rooms, another would build one with thirty-one guest rooms, and so on and so on.

William H. supplied two of his daughters, Margaret Louisa and Emily Thorne, with town houses on Fifth Avenue before he died.

My grandmother, Florence Adele Vanderbilt Twombly, outlived all her sisters.

She had a city house

and a country house,

and a house by the sea.

She had a husband, Hamilton McKown Twombly, who carried on the Vanderbilt tradition and added to it with his own investments,

and children: Ruth, Florence, Hamilton,

and Alice.

Alice died when she was twenty-three.

Hamilton drowned when he was counselor at a summer camp for poor boys.

Ruth did everything well.

MISS TWOMBLY IS A SKILFUL WHIP

Handles Her Father's Team of Steppers at Newport Like a Veteran.

DR. VES TO POLO GROUNDS

August Belmont, Alfred Vanderbilt and F. C. Havemeyer Among Those Who Play in Match.

[SPECIAL DESPATCH TO THE HERALD.]

NEWPORT, R. I., Saturday.—There was a crush of people at the polo grounds this afternoon to witness the practice game of polo, but the sensation of the occasion was Miss Ruth Twombly's artistic handling of four high steppers, harnessed to her father's coach. Miss Twombly, who has tooled a coach occasionally in the suburbs, under the direction of an instructor, brought the quartet into the ground with the skill and ease of a professional.

Miss Twombly's feat was a surprise even to her intimate friends, who know of her desire to become an accomplished whip, but who were not expecting to see her try her skill in a well filled carriage enclosure of a polo ground.
Hamilton Mc

Miss Ruth Twombly is a clever horsewoman, as every one knows, but she has even gained in skill during the last year. It is a pleasure to see her tool her coach-and-four along the Ocean Drive or down the avenue. Her experience on the hilly roads around "Florham," her father's estate in Madison, N. J., has given her great self-possession in handling the ribbons. On the polo grounds the other day Miss Ruth was a pretty picture as she sat on the box. She, as well as her girl friends on the coach, were all in white. Mrs. Twombly chaperoned the gay party. Miss Twombly is one of the most popular young women in Newport. She is much in demand, as while delightfully feminine, she is decidedly an outdoor girl, and "Vinland," Mr. H. McKay Twombly's house on the Cliffs, is the gathering place for all the young folk devoted to the strenuous outdoor life.

MISS TWOMBLY DRIVES FOUR-IN-HAND IN NEWPORT.

First Woman to Attempt the Feat in Public in the Fashionable Resort.

(Special to The World.)

NEWPORT, July 20.—During the driving hours to-day, between 4 and 6 P. M. everybody was out, including Mrs William Astor. At 5.30 a four-in-hand with the horses handsomely harnessed and with appointments perfect and up-to-date, dashed by the Casino. It was the first four-in-hand seen here this season and the ribbons were held by a pretty girl. It was the first four-in-hand ever driven in Newport by a woman in the fashionable driving hour. The whip was Miss Ruth Twombly, eldest daughter of Hamilton McKay Twombly. The young woman's superb driving attracted general attention.

LITTLE MISS TWOMBLY IN HER PONY CART. NEWPORT.

NEWPORT WELCOMES MISS TWOMBLY

Younger Daughter of Mr. and Mrs. H. McK. Twombly Makes Her Society Debut.

PLANS FOR SEPTEMBER

Mrs. Astor and Others, by Brilliant Dinner Parties, Will Try to Put Life Into the Season.

[SPECIAL DESPATCH TO THE HERALD.]

NEWPORT, R. I., Tuesday.—A pleasant incident of this busy day was the dinner and dance given to-night by Mr. and Mrs. H. McK. Twombly at Vinland, their villa on the Cliffs, for their second daughter, Miss Ruth Twombly, who will make her formal début in society next winter. The dinner company numbered seventy guests, who were seated at small tables. The floral decorations of the tables and of the various rooms of the villa came from the hothouses of Mr. Twombly.

After dinner there was a cotillon, Mr. Monson Morris leading with Miss Ruth Twombly. There were two bands of music, Mullalay's and Berger's, which played alternately for the dance. Numerous attractive favors were distributed, including taffeta work bags of different colors, brocade turnovers; rose sachets, heart boxes, clusters of forget-me-nots and pansies and silver trinkets.

Among those invited to the dinner were Mr. and Mrs. Alfred G. Vanderbilt, Mr. and Mrs. Reginald C. Vanderbilt, Mr. and Mrs. Philip M. Lydig, Mr. and Mrs. Elisha Dyer, Jr.; Mr. and Mrs. John R. Livermore, Mr. and Mrs. Lawrence M. Waterbury, Mr. and Mrs. Reginald Brooks, Mr. and Mrs. H. O. Havemeyer, Jr.; Mr. and Mrs. Peter D. Martin, the Misses Gladys Brooks, Janet Fish, Evelyn Burden, Gwendolyn Burden, Elsie Whelen, Mabel Gerry, Angelica Gerry, Laura Swan, Constance Livermore, Anita Sands, Beatrice Mills, Gladys Mills, May Van Alen, Therese Iselin, Nora Iselin, Mamie Pomeroy, Cynthia Roche, and Natalie Schenck; also the Messrs. Norman Whitehouse, Worthington Whitehouse, De Lancey Jay, Willing Spencer, I. Townsend Burden, Jr.; Francis J. Otis, Percy Wyndham, Francis Potter, Philip Potter, Marion Wright, Arthur Burden, Herman Norman, George McFadden, Cyril Hatch and Frederick C. Havemeyer.

Special to The New York Times.

NEWPORT, R. I., Aug. 18.—Mr. and Mrs. Hamilton McK. Twombly gave a dinner dance at Vinland to-night to introduce their younger daughter, Miss Ruth Vanderbilt Twombly. The affair had the Twombly mark of exclusiveness and was notable for its refinement rather than elaborateness and show. The dinner was served on five tables, each seating twelve persons, and each with its distinctive color, including white flowers for the débutante's table, and pink, yellow, dark, and light red for the others. The house was handsomely decorated with palms and cut flowers from the Vinland greenhouses, and the white-and-gold drawing room where the cotillion was danced had American Beauty roses banked on the mantels, with palms and potted plants massed in the corners. The cotillion was led by Munson Morris with Miss Twombly, and there were several favor figures, one of the most striking having handsomely decorated shepherd's crooks for the women and shepherd's horns for the men.

Vanderbilt Debutante.

MISS RUTH VANDERBILT TWOMBLY is t[h]e one Vanderbilt debutante of the season. S[he] has lots of money coming to her and h[as] already taken a place among the dashing femini[ne] four-in-hand whips. She is a nice, pleasant you[ng] woman, with many friends. Mr. and Mrs. H. McK[.] Twombly gave a preliminary dinner-dance for h[er] late in the season at Newport. Mrs. Vanderb[ilt,] Mrs. Sloane and Mrs. Webb will all give special fe[s]tivities in her honor, and she is likely to have mo[re] done for her than the other girls. If Mr. and M[rs.] William K. Vanderbilt and Mr. and Mrs. George Vanderbilt occupy their houses here as anticipat[ed,] Miss Twombly will have an unprecedented number [of] smart affairs given in her honor.

So did her sister Florence,
but she was more retiring.

One day William Armistead Moale Burden appeared.

His family owned the Burden Iron Company in Troy, New York.

They had the largest waterwheel in the world, and it was rumored they manufactured horseshoes for both the Union and Confederate armies during the Civil War.

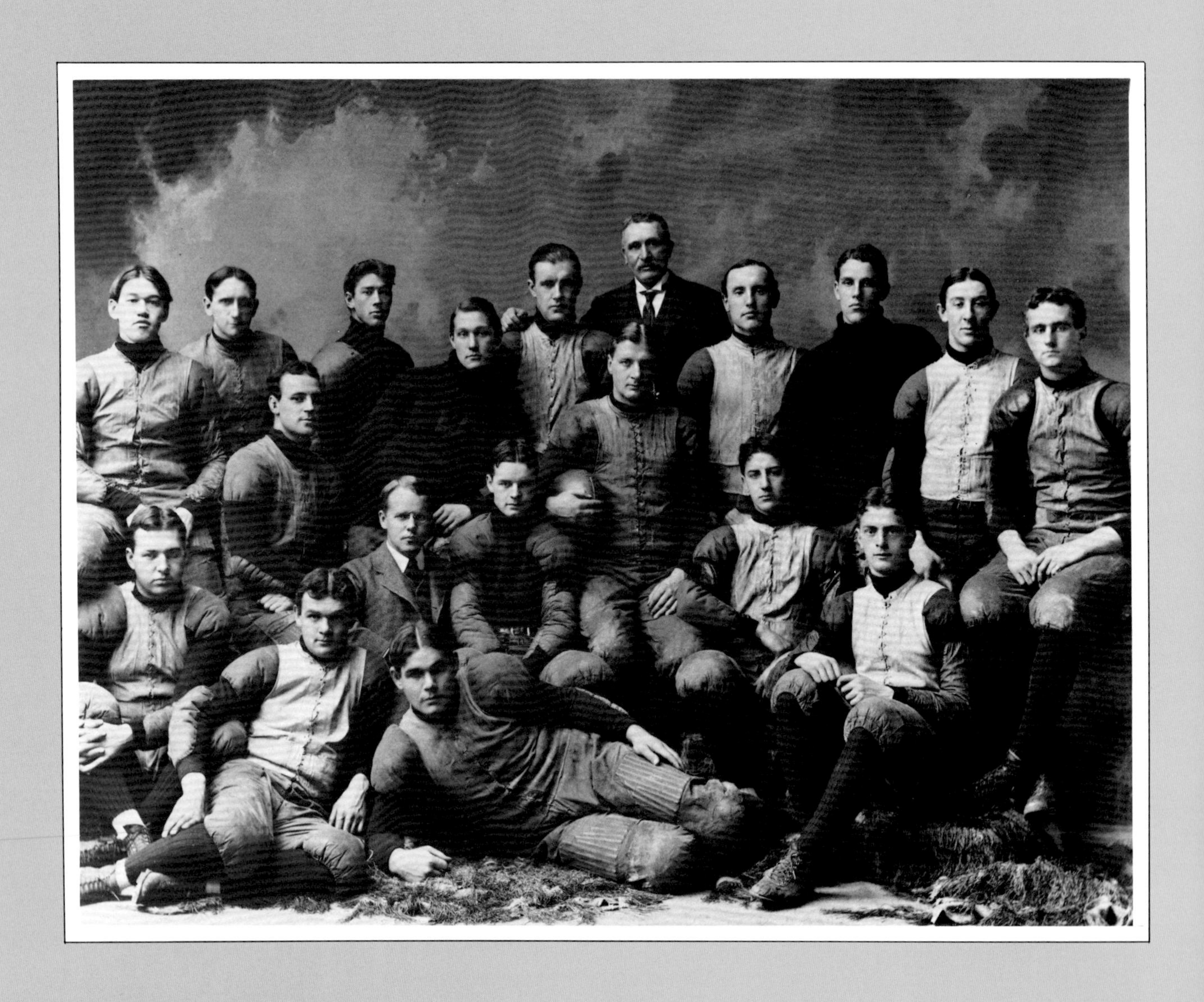

William was captain of the Harvard football team in 1900,

First Marshall of his class, and a member of

the A.D., Signet, and Hasty Pudding Clubs.

HASTY PUDDING CLUB.

He was the catch of the season. Everyone thought he would marry Ruth, but he didn't—

he fell in love with Florence.

New York American.
April-12-1904

TWOMBLY MARRIAGE GOWN A FORTUNE IN RICH LACES.

Granddaughter of the Vanderbilts Who Weds William A. Burden To-day Will Wear Most Artistic of Trousseaus

Miss Florence Vanderbilt Twombly, whose marriage to William A. M. Burden takes place at 3 o'clock this afternoon in St. Thomas's Church, will make an unusually handsome bride. A remarkably pretty girl, she will be attired in a gown of white satin, which will be a veritable work of art.

The lace that trims it, the finest of Brussels, is of cobwebby fineness and represents a small fortune in itself. The long trained skirt has three ruffles of this exquisite lace trimming it, draped with bunches of orange blossoms.

The bodice has a yoke of tulle, from which is arranged a bertha of the Brussels lace on which more orange blossoms are used. Miss Twombly will wear a superb veil of Brussels lace, which will be fastened with a wreath of orange blossoms.

The bride's sister, Miss Ruth Twombly, will be her maid of honor, and will wear a frock of white chiffon elaborately trimmed with Irish lace, and a white tulle hat with a similar garniture.

The bridesmaids, Miss Frederica Vanderbilt Webb, Miss Gwendolyn Burden, sister of the bridegroom; Miss Therese Iselin, Miss Pauline Robinson, Miss Cornelia Bryce and Miss Charlotte Jones, of Boston, will appear in frocks of light blue chiffon. These will also be trimmed with Irish lace, which will adorn their blue tulle hats. Miss Twombly has presented her attendants with turquoise and diamond pendants suspended from true-lovers bow knots of diamonds.

The reception, which takes place after the ceremony in the residence of the bride's parents, Mr. and Mrs. Hamilton McK. Twombly, No. 684 Fifth avenue, will be a large and elaborate affair. Sherry will serve the collation, and for this occasion his waiters will be dressed in knee breeches.

New York Telegram
April-12-1904

WILLIAM A. M. BURDEN WEDS MISS TWOMBLY

Ceremony Performed in St. Thomas' Church To-Day Unites Well Known Families.

William Armstead Moale Burden and Miss Florence Vanderbilt Twombly were married in St. Thomas' Church to-day by the Rev. Ernest M. Stires, rector of the church.

The interior was elaborately decorated. Tall palms filled the chancel, and on the altar were clusters of white roses which, in rope form and with festoons of smilax, also encircled the chancel rail. Yellow genestas and more white roses decorated the pulpit and Easter lilies in clusters were on the alternate pews.

Miss Twombly, whose father is Hamilton McKay Twombly, of No. 684 Fifth avenue, was preceded up the aisle by the following ushers:—Frank Higginson, Jr., James Lawrence, Jr., and John Saltonstall, of Boston; Rogers Winthrop, William Woodward, Charles Draper, Lewis Cass Ledyard, Jr., and William Post, of New York. The bridesmaids were the Misses Charlotte Jones, of Boston, and Frederica Webb, cousins of the bride; Gwendolyn Burden, sister of the bridegroom; Therese Iselin, Cornelia Bryce and Pauline Robinson. Miss Ruth Twombly was the maid of honor and I. Townsend Burden, Jr., the best man. Mr. and Mrs. Twombly gave the reception at their home.

Among the wedding gifts are a diamond corsage ornament and diamond bow knot, from two of her attendants, Miss Ruth Vanderbilt Twombly and Miss Frederica Webb; a diamond and emerald pendant from Mr. and Mrs. Frederick W. Vanderbilt, and a diamond pendant from William K. Vanderbilt.

This was the first wedding in the families of I. Townsend Burden and Hamilton McKay Twombly.

New York Press.
April-12-1904

The wedding of the week will be celebrated to-day, when Miss Florence Vanderbilt Twombly, daughter of Mr. and Mrs. H. McK. Twombly and granddaughter of William H. Vanderbilt, will become the bride of William A. M. Burden. The marriage will take place in St. Thomas's Church at 3 o'clock, and will be followed by a large reception in the residence of the bride's parents, No. 684 Fifth avenue.

They went to the Adirondacks on their honeymoon.

Their first child, Alice Twombly Burden, died when she was a month old.

My brother Bill came next,

and then me. They named me Shirley; just why I'll never know.

The house we lived in on Seventy-third Street in New York City is still standing. On the second floor there was a formal music room. I guess it was called a music room because there was a piano in it. Miss Weiss was my music teacher. When I look back on it I feel rather sorry for her. It took her two years of constant pounding to teach me to play "To a Wild Rose." At the end of each year she would gather her pupils around her and give a concert to prove to the parents that they weren't spending their money foolishly. I struggled through "To a Wild Rose," and was rewarded with a medal, of questionable metal, with my name engraved on it. Everybody was happy except the audience member who smiled sourly and whispered to a neighbor, "My child plays better than he does."

On the third floor there was a library with a desk, a Tiffany lamp, and lots of beautifully bound books. I was supposed to do my school homework at the desk with the Tiffany lamp. Instead I built a massive water bomb out of heavy brown paper and a pail of water. At the proper time I pushed it out of the window onto our mailman below. It didn't kill him but he got awfully wet.

On top of the stair railing leading from the third to the fourth floor, where my brother and I had our rooms, my mother had a heavy wire fence built to keep us from falling down the main stairwell. Bill and I soon found a way around that. The back stairs had absolutely no obstructions. It was a clear drop from the roof to the cellar.

Bill got a chemical set for Christmas. In it there was a formula for making German poison gas. I was rather timid about the idea but Bill went ahead and made it anyway and we used to drop it down the back stairs with fantastic success. My mother wondered why she lost so many maids.

That's my mother standing on the steps in black. She was in mourning for Dad, who died of leukemia in 1909 when I was a year old.

After Dad died my mother often took us to visit Grandma Twombly at Florham, her country house in New Jersey. The name is a combination of my grandmother's and grandfather's first names, Florence and Hamilton. We would take the Forty-second Street ferry to Weehawken and then drive to Madison. It was a long trip in those days. There were no freeways and no one hundred-mile-an-hour cars.

I'll never forget my first visit to Florham. I must have been seven or eight. We drove through a wonderful tunnel with trains on top, and down a driveway—

to the biggest house I had ever seen.

There were lions guarding the door,

and a hall that had no end; thirty-six bedrooms,

and living rooms for everything.

A thousand acres to play in.

But you can't play in the playhouse.

You can't play in the Orangerie.

You can't play in the greenhouses.

You can't play at the farm.

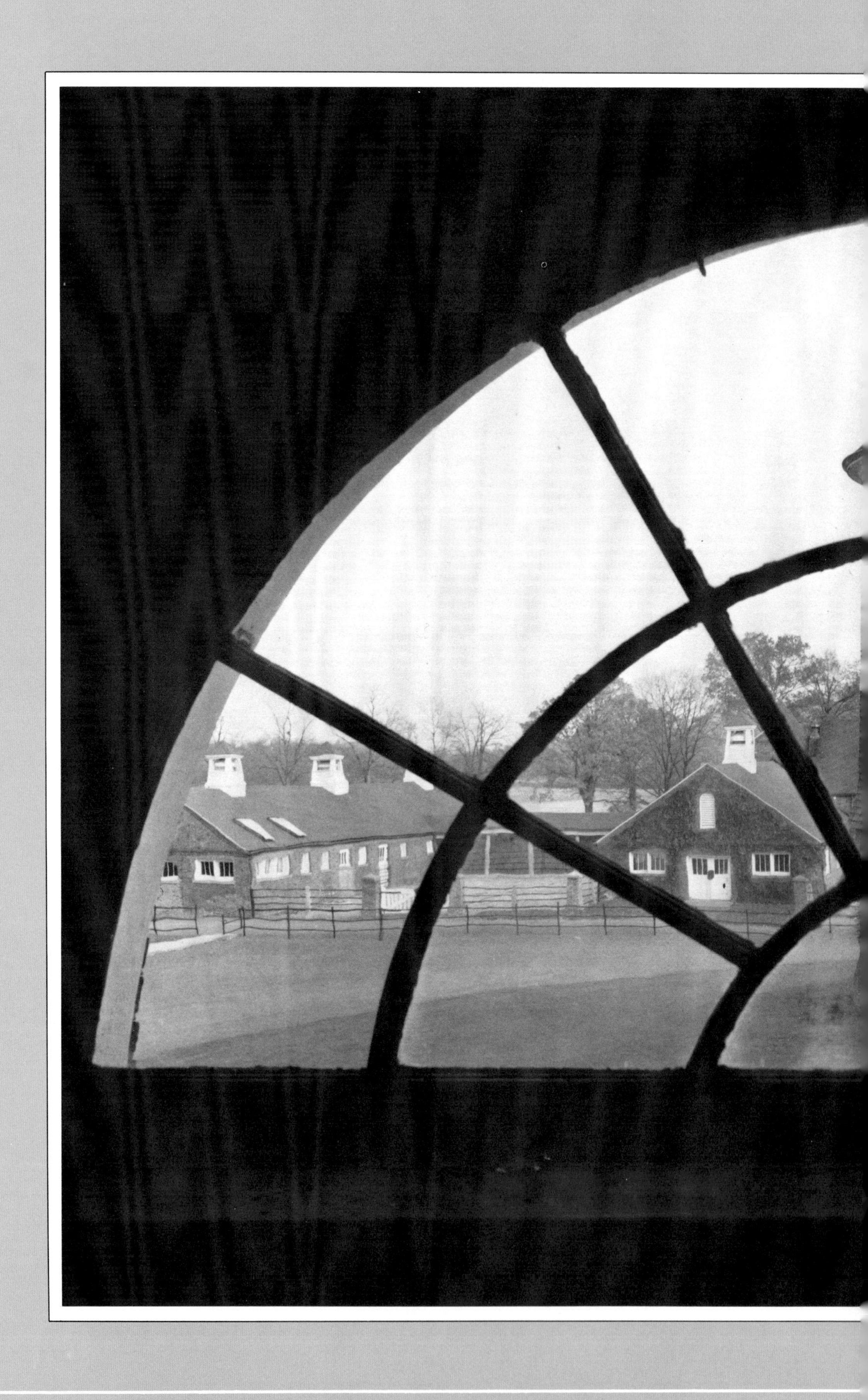

You can't play at the stable.

So we played in the leaves.

When Grandma died, so did Florham.

Aunt Ruth loved Paris. In 1900, when she was very young, she brought home these pictures of the Paris Exposition. It must have been a wonderful show.

In 1954 Aunt Ruth and a friend of hers decided they wanted to see Paris again:

They wanted to stay at the Ritz Hotel on the Place Vendôme—

They wanted to have a drink at the Ritz Bar—

They wanted to have lunch in one of those wonderful restaurants in the Bois de Boulogne—

They wanted to go to the horse races—

They wanted to buy the latest French fashions—

They wanted to window-shop on the rue St. Honore—

They wanted—

C'EST
QUI N'APPARTIENT

Aunt Ruth died there. At the Ritz.

RITZ
HOTEL

DANGER
KEEP CLEAR
PROPELLERS

My mother, my brother, and I went to Paris to bring back her body. The voyage home on the S.S. *United States* wasn't a very comfortable one for poor Aunt Ruth. Her trip from Paris to Cherbourg, where the *United States* was docked, was made in a Volkswagen bus, which is quite different from a Rolls Royce. I watched as they hoisted her coffin aboard. It was soon lost in the darkness. When I entered our cabin my mother and my brother were staring into space. I joined them. My mother was the first to speak. "Where did they put Aunt Ruth?" she asked. "I don't know, Moms," I answered. "Please find out where she is," she said.

A steward took me somewhere on the ship; I don't know exactly where. The vibration was terrible. He opened a small door and motioned me in. I felt as if I was in an empty football field. Walls of steel surrounded me. Above there were shining chrome bars and above them, a small patch of blue sky. Below there were more bars and more bars and the noise of pounding engines. I was inside one of the ship's funnels. There were no crates, no machines, no people to warm the scene—just emptiness, vibration, and noise. In the center of the funnel a small brown casket was lashed to the bars.

I went on deck and watched the waves for a while before I returned to our cabin. As soon as I opened the door my mother said, "Is she all right, is she all right?"

I walked to the porthole and watched the waves again. "She's fine, Moms," I said.

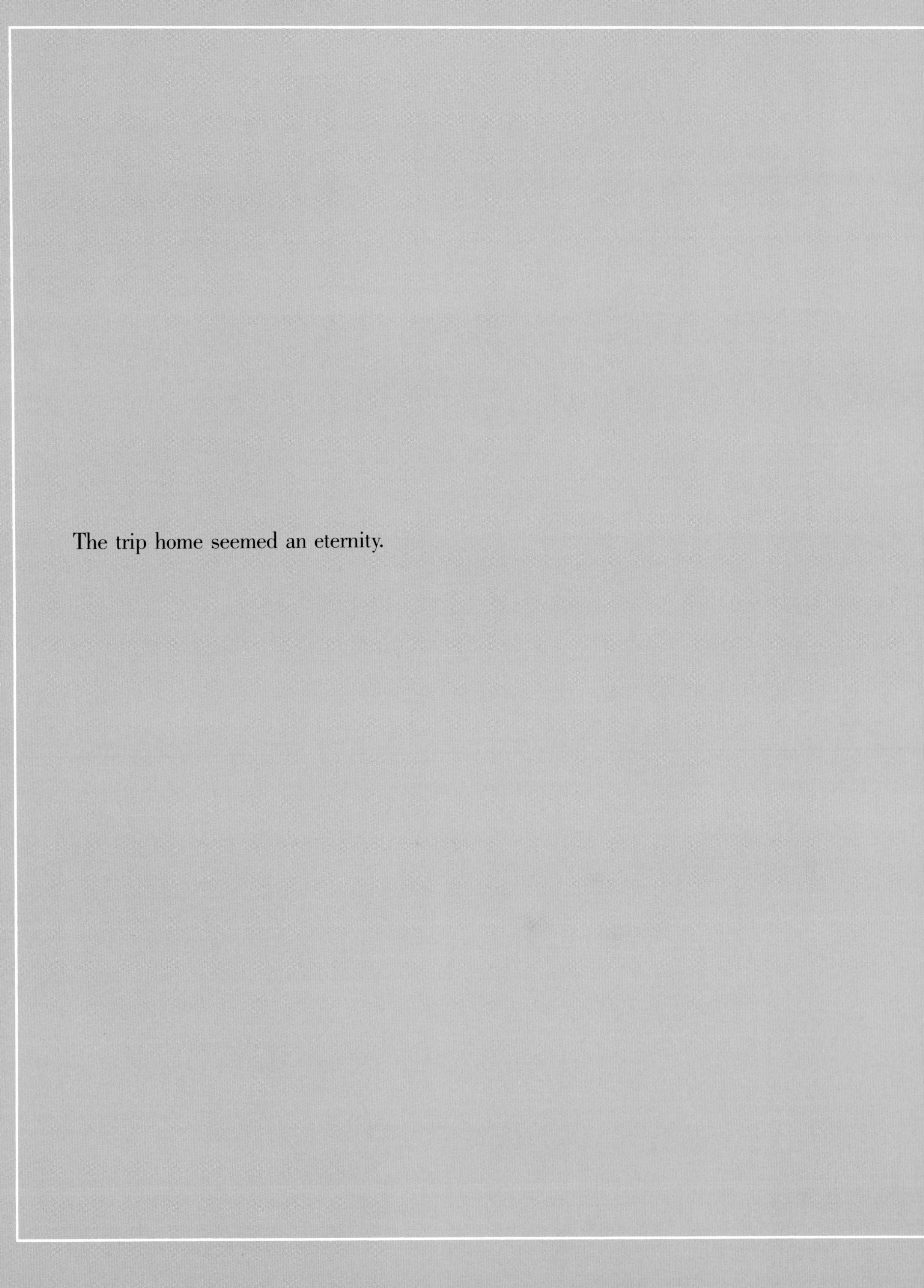

The trip home seemed an eternity.

I, Ruth V. Twombly, being of sound and disposing mind and memory, do hereby make, publish and declare the following, my last will and testament.

My mother, my brother, and I were the only ones left now.

Twenty-two million dollars.

Twenty-two million.

Then the government took eighteen million.

There were conferences,
and conferences,
and more conferences.

Heirlooms were divided,

expenses cut,

fifty years of loyal service.

I wondered what would happen to the three men who did nothing but rake the gravel drives; to McFadyen, the head gardener, and his thirty men who nursed the orchids and manicured the grounds; to the man who always chased me and then snitched to my mother when I stole strawberries; to Allen, who was in charge of the farm, and his twelve men, who fed and milked and washed and polished the prize herd of thirty guernsey cows until they shone like gold; to Frederick, the head butler, who always greeted us at the front door at Florham; to the two men that did nothing but polish silver, and the man that washed dishes all day, and the four footmen who woke you up, served you breakfast, lunch, and dinner, pressed your clothes and drew your bath; to the eight maids who cleaned and dusted the forty bedrooms and twenty-five bathrooms with wood-burning fireplaces, the two dining rooms, and four living rooms, and that long hall that had no end. What would happen to Monsieur Donnen, *chef par excellence*, culinary artist of the century, and his four assistants? What would happen to the full-time painters, bricklayers, and furniture repairmen who kept Florham looking like new; to the twelve men who watched over Vinland and the wonderful Belgian grapes they raised there; to Grandma's chauffeur and footman, who opened and closed the door when Grandma got in or out of the car; to Aunt Ruth's chauffeur and footman; to the man who did nothing but wash their cars? What would become of them? Then there was Miss Curry, Grandma's housekeeper, who tried to keep one hundred and twenty-six employees happy.

Would there be anybody to care for the little room with the bench under the terrace near the rose garden where they kept the croquet set?

Would the fires that once warmed Florham turn to ashes?

H. MCK. TWOMBLY
1909

Would the generators that flooded Florham with light give only darkness?

I just wanted to say goodbye.

My brother Bill, like the Commodore and William H. Vanderbilt, is a business man. He graduated from Harvard with honors, was a member of the A.D. Club, worked on Wall Street and for the Defense Department, was Ambassador to Belgium.

I guess I was different—I never got into Harvard. I remember when I went to the Columbia University gymnasium with nine hundred other guys to take a preliminary college entrance examination. I was too busy watching the sparrows flying around the gymnasium ceiling to answer any of the questions. I tried for two years and then decided to go west to find fame and fortune in the motion picture industry.

GENOVA

I found neither, but I found a wonderful wife. When I went to Hollywood all my mother's dear friends told her, "You'd better watch out, or he will marry some blonde motion picture actress." Well, they were right. Flobelle was blonde, she was an actress, she was Douglas Fairbanks, Sr.'s niece, and on top of it all, she was a blind date. Luckily though, I wasn't blind. Her death was the only thing that separated us, thirty-five years later. Flobelle is next to Douglas Fairbanks, Sr.

We had two children,
Muff and Carter.
The dog was extra.

Carter went into politics.

Muff got married in her grandmother's wedding dress and her great-grandmother Twombly's wedding veil.

The Vanderbilt family tree has grown and prospered since the Commodore was born on May 27, 1794. The houses that the Vanderbilt girls built haven't fared so well: One East Seventy-first Street is an apartment house; Florham is a branch of Fairleigh Dickinson University; Florham Farm is an Esso experimental laboratory; Vinland is a Catholic girls' school.

A way of life has gone, a new one is here, and still another is just around the corner.